Essential Poets Series 52

Yves Préfontaine

This Desert Now

Translated from the French
by Judith Cowan

Guernica

Montreal, 1993

Original Title:
Le Désert maintenant

© Yves Préfontaine and Les Écrits des Forges, 1987.
© Yves Préfontaine and L'Hexagone, 1990.
Translation © Judith Cowan and Guernica Editions Inc., 1993.
All rights reserved.
Typeset and printed in Canada.
Cover conception by Julia Gualtieri.
Cover design by Gianni Caccia.

15/2/95

Antonio D'Alfonso, editor.
Guernica Editions Inc.
P.O. Box 633, Station N.D.G.
Montreal (Quebec), Canada H4A 3R1

The Publisher gratefully acknowledges financial assistance from The Canada
Council and Le Ministère des Affaires culturelles du Québec.

Legal Deposit — Second Quarter
National Library of Canada and Bibliothèque nationale du Québec.

Canadian Cataloguing in Publication Data

Préfontaine, Yves, 1937-
(Désert maintenant. English)
This desert now

(Essential poets; 52)
Translation of: Le désert maintenant.
ISBN 0-920717-66-7

I. Cowan, Judith Elaine II. Title. III. Désert maintenant. English.
IV. Series.

PS8531.R43D4713   1992   C841'.54   C92-0900
PQ3919.2.P74D4713   1992

Table of Contents

II
This Desert Now

Preface

There is a well-known, well-worn Italian saying which would have us believe that translations are always traitors to their originals. And although this centuries-old cliché does contain a grain of truth, it also conveys considerable ambiguity.

Even if no translator, however brilliant, can ever transmit the whole of the rhythm, the music, the scansion of the original, it is still equally true that in the best cases the translation may be transmuted into a genuine re-creation of the original, which is thus reborn, once or several times, like a phoenix of music and thought. And for this to happen a special sort of love relationship must bloom between the translator and the work of the author, an involvement that goes beyond mundane professional or technical considerations. Obviously this is beyond the function of technical translators who exercise their professional skills coldly, in accordance with their varying degrees of competence. Literary translation is different; literary translation is generally a labour of love. There are even examples of translations — like Baudelaire's translation of Edgar Allan Poe — where the translation is reputed to surpass the original. This I have heard myself from the lips of American *littérateurs*, whose indifference to their 'great' compatriot had always been a source of puzzlement to me, considering the extent of his influence on the second half of the nineteenth century in France. I am thinking too of Stéphane Mallarmé's translations of Poe, which gave them a sharpness and a crystalline density not to be found in the English, or of Marguerite Yourcenar's translations of Virginia Woolf, so close to the heights of the original.... Not all of us are literary giants, however, nor do all translation projects succeed.

An example of the besetting obstacles is to be found in the following sad little tale. In 1980, when the only translations of my work to have appeared were short pieces in magazines and anthologies, I found in my mail one day, from a perfect stranger in Vancouver, the complete translation of a work which had appeared in 1970, in the middle of the October crisis: *Débâcle*, followed by *À l'orée des travaux*. This was all the more astonishing because the book was far from being my best known. I had long hoped for a translation of some of my works — perhaps of the book that it amuses me to describe as my 'best-seller', *Pays sans parole* — and the possibility had been discussed from time to time but had somehow never come to fruition. Then all the way from Vancouver came the translation of a book which I had thought long submerged by the shock waves following the War Measures Act. (At this point I should say that, although I am certainly not an English-language specialist, I can and do read the language with pleasure and with an awareness of its rhythms — so much more pronounced than those of French — and of its special musicality. There was a period of my life when, with the French translation beside the English,

I read Gerard Manley Hopkins with fascination. So faced with a translation of my own poems, I do feel a certain confidence in my ability to detect imprecisions and to suggest corrections likely to help the translator.) Unfortunately, however, through my own negligence or disorganization, I lost contact with that first translator. I tried repeatedly to retrace him and never succeeded, although we had exchanged letters and talked on the telephone. Beyond all considerations of political stupidity or deep-rooted prejudice, our so-called country is just too big and Vancouver is too far away. Sometimes I still take his translation out of my filing cabinet and read the poems over. I think about them and tell myself again that this should have been a book. If anyone out there knows him, please tell him to write to me. His name was Sandy McIlwain. But I see that I am digressing.

This more recent intellectual adventure, the translation of *Le Désert maintenant* with Judith Cowan, has had a much happier ending, for the simple reason that she has chosen to live in Québec and to teach at the Université du Québec à Trois-Rivières. And even if certain existential considerations place Trois-Rivières almost as far from Montreal as Vancouver is, there is nevertheless a difference.

Judith and I first met at the Festival International de la Poésie in Trois-Rivières, probably in 1986. Unlike other English-Canadian scholars, writers and translators, she knew absolutely nothing of my work or of my place in the literary and political panorama that is Québec — just as I knew nothing of

9

her writings or her work as a translator. And strangely, this was a wonderful thing because it meant that in the cultural sense, we were both virgins. She was the charming small-town university professor living in a welter of books (except, through some fluke of fate, mine) and it was precisely in Trois-Rivières, in the spring of 1987, that Les Écrits des Forges was to publish *Le Désert maintenant*, which, up until the publication of my retrospective in 1990, was my most recent book. Only Judith can say whether her encounter with *Le Désert* was a literary *coup de foudre* or a simple exercise. She began by offering, casually, to translate a couple of poems. I thought we had left it at that, so I was surprised, only a month and a half after the launching of the book, to receive a short letter from her, dated the 23rd of June (the eve of our Fête Nationale, interestingly enough) in which she said,

Bonjour Yves Préfontaine,

Herewith my translations of four of your poems. I am hoping that you will like them. Your handling of words is not easy to imitate in the other language and I do not really know if the translations are any good... but they were an interesting challenge.

Sincerely,
Judith Cowan

Well, what I found myself reading was more than just good. Her translations *rendered* the meaning of the original as I had rarely felt it in my previous experiences with translation. And what I still had not realized was that, without saying anything, Judith was going to spend the following winter translating the whole book. Thus an even greater surprise was to follow when, a few months later, the complete translation arrived.

Once I had recovered from my astonishment, I made a careful and thorough reading of the 'baby'. Judith had accomplished the essential. In a way, it was now *her* creation as much as mine. After that we went over it together, minutely, several times, and in the process I learned much of the twists and turns and traps, the Sargasso Sea that awaits the translator. Often her translation succeeds in transmitting not just the rhythm but the actual intimacy, the *juice* of the original. But then would come a break, a *rupture*, when the spirit of the language would suddenly fail. Sometimes we had to find long periphrases to translate a line of just a few words whose sonority was *immanent* to their meaning. Or passages transposed into the other language would all at once seem trivial phonically, or somehow lame when compared with the music of the original, with the sound-and-sense osmosis which is the foundation of the text.

We had long discussions, traded suggestions back and forth, engaged in laborious negotiations between the spirits of two different languages... and sometimes I succeeded in elucidating Judith's text. But most of the time she was right. The problems of translation are ineluctable. One tries to improve the text, word by word and line by line, and then runs up against an immovable obstacle, a complex of problems involving the sound-and-sense equivalence, the central matrix from which all 'true' poetry is born. It is here that arises, like a sharp, terrible suffering, the realization that never, never, will the *other* who does not know my language be able to grasp the full scope, the music, the real impact of the 'inner spheres', I tried so hard to communicate, or my vision of the world and of existence, my style, my quest, my personal ontology, my striving towards communion.

This is the anguish of the creator, however, and it should not be allowed to detract from the merit of the translator, who went through the same agonies of choice and decision, and whose intellectual prowess ought to figure on the honours list of some Olympics of creation.

And finally, there is one memory associated with this translation which I should like to record. I have an old, old friend who has lived in Trois-Rivières forever, and whose all-too-rare publications once had, in the 1940s, the force of lightning bolts slicing through the gray mists that were the Québec publishing world of that time. He was a friend of my father's and he became my friend; it was he who published my third book, *L'Antre du poème*, in 1960; he was the first publisher of Gérald Godin, among others. This man, Clément Marchand, is the sort of cultivated man of letters one no longer meets anywhere, civilized to the tips of his fingers.

Living in retirement (and with good reason) in what urban intellectuals are pleased to disdain as 'the provinces', Clément has long been an intellectual lighthouse, shining with a steady, far-reaching light, infinitely clearer than that of any flashy urban fabricator. In Trois-Rivières he has surrounded himself with a rich library and a collection of paintings and engravings lovingly chosen, more often with a view to helping a starving artist than from any desire to invest in the art market. And it was, during the 1990 Festival de la Poésie, that Judith and I were invited to his house on the Boulevard des Forges, into that book-lined retreat which he rarely leaves. He offered us wine, and we started to read aloud, each in turn, from her translation and my original. Then the miracle occurred: two citizens of this land breaking down, word by word, in the velvet silence of Clément Marchand's library, all the angry pride, the incomprehension, and the dull and stupid soliloquies that have been the distinguishing characteristic of our peoples' history for the last two centuries.

We read on into the small hours of the morning and I think we read the whole book, interrupted often by exclamations from Clément — enthusiastic, passionate, pertinent, *loving*. It was an extraordinary evening of intense communion between three people touched by a moment of rare grace, a genuine poetic grace which carrried us far from the pettiness and the infamy, the physical and moral violence of the outside world. Although poetry remains aware of all that. The role of poetry is to bear witness. In times of emergency, that is its primary role. As time passes, it becomes more and more urgent to choose between the light and the darkness. And at this moment of my life, I have chosen the light. But for how long? Who can say?

It remains only for me to thank Judith for the gift she made to me when she so generously undertook this work. It is one of the best presents I have ever received.

Yves Préfontaine
Montreal and Philipsburg, August 1991

I

IN THE ROAR OF REALITY

Frontispiece

*For D.G. Jones, this first text written
here in Québec, at his house in North
Hatley, after a silence which had
possessed me for months and after my
return to our wonderful homeland of
the War Measures Act and of lost
friendships....*

I

To rend this opacity, suddenly, I mean us, the silence of
ancient roots now turned to stone.

To rend open— as birth breaks the female in a flow-
ering of pain and leafy ecstasies.

May the fertile earth invade the rock or I shall die....

Water teaches me its memory and light opens to me
its knowledge and the mystery of its lasting....

I will learn nothing more that is not closest to ger-
mination.

And I want no other masters than April between
snow and fern.

*T*o rend asunder—

like any beginning, as much man with his primal abrasions as a star torn from a welter of syllables.

Song will never serve again to mark the measure of a time of certainty.

Did song ever take place? And will it again?

I waited so long for the sowing, but also for the scattering of a necessary chaos.

I imprinted upon my path the sense of a faint clarity glimpsed somewhere and which I must set aside again.

At times I dreamed that there might appear again in haughty theatre the dead solemnity of a speech of inscrutable splendour.

But speech in action is born of a sundering.

And I am naming the gap between genesis and completion.

To rend, certainly, but above all to carry forward, the same roots of a language either too new or already lost.

April 1971.

Pollen

I

I am returning from so far away,
leaving a life of ellipsis lived in the fury of men.

I find I am obliged to name each thing again,
to find for it its place again
in order to learn once more how far it is that I have come
and the savour of time.

II

An eternity of ice   one winter too many.

But now there is a clarity that rings from the new
surfaces of things.
Dark until now, this instant is refined into a light
bright enough to be mistaken for noon.

Soon sun and soil will find their way
towards a proliferation of warm forces.

This is a friendship between the insects   the sand
the water although still cold
and my sick words naming them and summoning
them with love.

This is only the blind old earth once more
        and yet the single certitude
in the night exploded now with all the pollens
        fables of summer.

III

A stone spoke to me
and I did not hear.

Stunted life
with dying root.

In the noise,
in the warlike noise made by the men with the
        narrow faces,
in the noise,
        the rumblings of predator nations,
I had come to hear only the worn surfaces of days
        spent in the clash of arms.

But returning to the primaeval pollen,
to the barely flickering fires of true speech,
I may yet find again the stone that spoke to me.

IV

For all things are speech
and speech is pollen
for the beauty of a burgeoning.

Silence   The Effacing of Signs

I

Like this pathway to the internal star
where one loses one's way in the thorns.

And all at once the wound which was thought
to be mortal
is vested with light.

And certainly the wound is mortal.

But the light ever farther ahead
draws us onward confronting death.

II

I know nothing.
I have learned nothing
in spite of tears and blind labours.

But I am slowly learning earthly taste
and the breadth of what remains.

III

Sharp stones....

Who goes there?

There nothing is possible
but only mirage or real knowledge of the undreamed.

I can hear my blood pulsing in the cold rock.

IV

Splendour of far-flung clarities
over what remains of half-wintered earth.

The North, the North explodes in the chilling tree.
The North explodes in the blood of light that bursts
    my eye.

V

I see   blind   I see now
    the essence of clarities so near to the gods.
I see as if between two stars the far-reaching gyrations
    of parabolas and parables.

Splendour without a name.

Such quantities of light are dissolving within my body
and my open palms quiver
    with an impossible offering.

I see nothing and I see everything,
blind dazzled in the silence of musics
    beginning again forever their self-pursuit,
yet finding at the end of themselves only
that splendour without a name, either noun or verb,
of the light which in itself inhabits me and yet
    does not
since I am no longer here.

VI

Light,
homeland of force.

I seek it in the very heart,
the heart of stones,
in other stonelike things,
and in dead things.

Light,
mother of words proffered by worlds
and of the birthless view from the other side of time.

Light.
I seek it
with the stubbornness of a man who cannot rest,
the stubbornness of the round stone
and the love of the pollen which is nothing
    without it.

I seek it and can no longer find it
beneath so much ice.

Winter is in the soul.

Winter is in the soul.

And the sun is lost in its last sleep.

VII

That which I know collides with the uproar of men.

But that which I know accords

   with the silence

      of those who see

         the effacing of signs.

Black Spruce Black

*For Gilles Vigneault, in memory of
our first meetings some centuries ago,
this prose piece written in his country,
the Lower North Shore, which I love
almost as much as he does... and a
different way of singing.*

Also for my friend, Régine Nantel.

I

If I had to lose myself again in the back country of
my Gemini birth — for a thick layer of forgetfulness
had dimmed it to my sight — would I then rediscover
my first obedience to the sea and the red of these
rocks?

Behind me the island of childhood in its green-
ness bears witness to the vast length of time still
stretching to my door. And before me, can it be that
the future resembles the archipelagoes of the first
sun...?

To be born to one's own luminous death amidst the hardships and the sweetnesses.

To be born to the very odour of clarity which germinates towards and against so many winters.

And thus to be born into the cold of the world is to join that glimmer lost in darkness where are born and grow unceasingly both languages and forms.

Black spruce black to the infinity of this terraqueous leaf-mould, I learn again the bitterness, the breadth, the hollow rooty resonance of the spaces where cling the fragile lichens of my words.

III

I no longer know where ancient languages go, precious dust-motes of a dying light in the beauty of slow shipwreck.

I no longer know where the primal rhythms have gone, that gave me birth and nourished me with the food of fable. In what upheaval were lost the phantoms of my nameless navigations.

I no longer know what thunder has been lost. For I was using words to make the snake-haired lightning last. And I knew it.

And I no longer know where the gemstones have gone, that took fire at the very instant my eyes sought out the flame.

All lost now in the sickness of cities, my stones, my trees, the ancient song swelling from the depths of undertow.

I no longer know where I cast my anchor or how often.
I no longer know what I know.

But I hold for certainty the substance of the sun upon the sands of my skin.

IV

When did I lose sight of myself, and for what desert have I forgotten the stretch of my thirst?

In what root shall I find myself again and for how long, amidst the living fruit and the high winds?

Shall I be, in its blackness alone, like the black spruce in endless blackness, or, like the spruce, spiked with claws with a view to surviving?

Is not stone long softened by the sea and stone on fire nevertheless still stone?

Why must I in an instant die to the speech that names me?

V

If I cannot learn again the wound and the sun, then I know nothing.

And I no longer knew anything, abandoned by the forces, by the grass and the winds.

I was losing my way in the uproar and the mirage and the glittering ruins.

But here once more is the storm of the fables, tearing me away from the sepulchre of noise.

Dissolved and reduced,
hampered in the absolute prolongation of my
gestures,
haunted by great dead birds and unknown
animals come from far distances,
I flickered out in the rasp of a black laugh.

Being mad for the sun saved me from the end.

But here I am taking up the course of things as one catches one's breath at the end of roads and navigations.

In Natashquan, July 21, 1973.

TILL THE END OF THE SUN

Till the End of the Sun

To Louise Houde, in spite of every-
thing, for the longest time of serenity
and happiness which it has been my
lot to know.

My soul burnt out in lost wars
does not overflow with any boundless melting,
nor am I the bread given without return,
nor did I ever learn the patience of the seasons.

But through and beyond pain and disaster
your breath reached me, stayed with me.
Today I flame up where your roots reach down to
     drink
and I turn from the cold where I was sinking in frozen
     raptures.

I knew that plunged in the hearts of hard stones
there hid a humus touching ancient memories,
and long I lived with bygone rites
ringing with primal chants and rhythms.
I lived from the cold of my fables till the end
     of that cold.

I knew I was lost but my anger was stronger.

If now the undertow grows weaker,
I still have not forgotten nor ever shall forget
its nourishing resonance.

When even for a wild grass, a volcano was my prayer-
chant.

When even for a woman mingled with ferns
the sense in me would tear away
in a flood-tide of words.

Neither my war nor my tears can ever testify
to those vigils and those murders.
For today the Word is growing in the shadow of the
eclipse.

I knew nothing anymore that was not close to the
gods.
But cities and the weight of the species
dragged me down and downwards with their noise.

I knew nothing anymore that was not close to the
origins,
oh close as the very waters come close to rhythm....

And a number dissolved among numbers,
I crumbled away in broken bits, revelations glimpsed
only to find myself once more amongst angels with
gnawed masks
and the stone claw-marks of a half-dead planet.

Oh, how lost I was already although my anger was
    stronger.

I went forward, hampered, in the midst of my war
    and my tears.
And I am walking still, going I know not where.

But I know of a fire that lasts, lasts as long
    as the cold of all time.
I know now of a harder fire
        than the longest stretch of all duration.
And the sun tells me that I am right to survive
if I knot into my days the link and the soul
    of your hands.

Infinitely I flame up and always shall flame up
in the place where your roots, which have become
    mine,
        mingle and drink.

And my thirst will not be staunched till the end of
    the sun.

Words that Everyone Always Says

Words,
words spoken every day by everyone,
and I, amongst the spectres   I shouted them
     out still unaware.
I shouted them out to any woman with langorous looks.

And   a spectre to myself   I hollowed out forms,
and wrought great raucous chants,
and exhausted myself in very ancient wars,
     forgotten rituals.

Words.
Ceaselessly I shouted out words.

And I crawled   familiar of thorns and
     exploded countries
     where no one lingers,
I crawled in the shadow of a shadow filled with
     knives,
and I crawled beneath winds blacker still blacker
     than the very thickness of absence,
and I crawled to the clinging water that resembles
     you.

Words.
The words   *I love you*
and I do not want to die far from your hands
     for that would be dying twice.

THE THICKNESS OF THIS TIME
THE LASTING OF THIS COLD

Poems of Circumstance

The Night of November 15, 1976

I

White snowdrop in November
I gleam with a fire
a new flowering under the ice.

I am returning from so far away,
I am returning from cold so dense,
that never could I put into words
the thickness of that time
or the lasting of that cold.

Snowdrop clinging to the rock
and lost in the wastes of lichen,
I know how rare the good earth is
and I learn again that light persists
where speech is born
in the speech of the other,
in the warmth, the signal-call and the laughter
through the hard and vanquished night.

White snowdrop in November
I shall go now towards winter
my free soul flowering with harvests.

II

What to say of the night
when we were incised
as in a destiny of stones.

What to say of the night
when we dug ever deeper
our enormous wound.

What to say of the absence
— of the faded speech
— of our ruined faces.

What to say of a day
which died without a cry
in the uproar all around.

And what to say of the silence.

III

White snowdrop in November,
I shall go now towards winter
with my soul free,
sharing those rays of light and of staying-power,
the human face of all our strengths.

*Written in the night following
the victory of the Parti Québécois.*

Mourning

I hear it.
A cold thunder rumbling
        in the deepest marrow of my bones,
the angry torrent still growling under the ice.

Oh, how I hear you, sneering ruins
        over this contemptible people,
repeating again the news of disaster and shame.
I hear again as before the tattered shreds of our dreams
        snapping in the wind.
I hear again as before the pulsing seduction of despair
        and speechlessness.

But I shall never hear a word of the language of the
        master,
        or of the traitor to himself.
I will hear nothing of refusals.
I impugn the mirage as much as my cry turned against
        itself.

I wager my life against the forces of darkness,
and I know I shall lose. But still I wager.
When I know that I shall lose,
for encrusted in us still I see the eye of the masters
        and the eye of the order that feeds them.

And louder than ever before I hear, howling with
        terror,

the pack enraged by the slightest bud
that opens to grow in freedom.

So faced with all that I see and foresee,
I hear as well, growling in the depths of my veins —
an icy ardour.

> *Written in the night of the twentieth*
> *of May, 1980, following the referendum*
> *on sovereignty-association.*

CHINA 1977

China, 1977

I

You conquer the dust, the ruins and time, men of
the loess.
Your smiles imbue the very word of desert.

Here one chant thrills through the mingled veins of
men and soil.

And shall we learn to link hands across hate and
weapons,
and shall we learn the depths of the space in the
centre of each,
and shall we learn the new warmth of the sun, men
of the loess,
and will we travel farther still despite the chill
that reigns in our narrow souls?

II

We are too far from the sap of the tree
and the lovely temples are lost since long
in the fog of earth's end.

Poverty, its hammered wretchedness
had never struck to the centre of my life.

And I had seen nothing.

For I sprang from a land where the traces of man were
        no more
than the October passage of the birds,
where I could wander in space and the dream of grass.
No horror turned its blade in my people's wounds like
        this,
and I knew nothing of peoples whose wounds
        were real
nor of their livid terror.

We mistook the real assassins
        when we spoke of men.
We mistook the real assassins.

The absolute delirium of orderly machines had
        drugged us.
We found ourselves in the wrong country.

The wars took place.
They were images and symbols and far away.

And we dreamed of gardens.

For others the cadence of the murder of the species,
while we offered to the sun our heedless skins.

But the fear of fading pleasure now flickers low
in the hot and terrible accretion of numbers

and the need is revealed, the unplumbed need behind
       this fracas of waving flags.

We must change faces.

Our eyes open suddenly upon the force of children.

III

I shall remember men
in a galaxy of yellow wind
and their numbers.
I shall remember an enormous smile
in the barbarous rictus of this time.
And I shall remember my snows dissolved
      in the eternity of the loess.
A billion hands waving in the primal work
      of survival.

For too long I lost my way in the weightlessness
      of words.
But I shall return.
I shall return to this side of the earth
     where the soul grows taller
        by falling silent
          and listening.

Written in the train between
Sian and Luoyang, February 1977.

Return from China

O_{cean,}
ellipsis of forces.
Ocean of men, so much closer to the threshold.

Have we been summoned to the celebration of light
    or to the orgies of death?

From Vancouver, looking
back towards Asia.

THE VERY ESSENCE OF SONG

Anton Webern

After thirty-five years of listening

Barely stroking the senses, the essence of song
as if in approach to primal silence,
with the soul naked — stripped.

Preceding the sound of being,
then proceeding from the sound of being,
as if to say the sap,
the measured madness both stern and sweet
that underlies
this precisely structured shiver.

Never to speak just for talking,
never to sing but to the brink
of love and clarity.
Never to express but the most perfect thought
        of the tree,
heart of things.

To be, absolutely.

To be the very being of music,

my food and my hunger both.

John Coltrane

Ten years after his death

and also for the very great Aimé Césaire

Beauty
of a blackness of negro sun
     exploded in the ultimate roar
       rut of death

of androgynous blackness
         flowers of sound
Yesterday and tomorrow
     I remember
     (Oh how I remember, in my country which
     remembers nothing)

I remember well   how well in the night
        our bodies
     porous with music and good
     in the warmth of your breath

You saturated space
and the fibres of our lives
demiurge
     negro
         dead at the front twice rather than once
         dead in the torment of *telling all*
           at the frontiers of cry

I loved you   you never knew   you never
I loved you more than poem or speech
        dead grasses
        facing the torrent of your signs

Coltrane-my-friend-pure-negative-of-my-snow-white-
        photo
misery of ebony as in the Stravinsky concerto
for petty bourgeois figuring their fractions of guilt
on the Stock Market of horror

Beauty
        slaughtered god
                black misery *without limits*
                        like the slave-trading sea

What I loved in you
        was the very essence of song
        breaking down the executioners
although the executioner survived

God-negro-America   a bitter marmalade
And you   you, your too-brief wizardry stopped
        short   like that
as if you had nothing more to say   you
        Love Supreme

And I weep   Trane
I am your own blues ringing out for help 'Naïma'
for help 'Africa' and I refuse   and refuse again
                despite time mocking me

your death and my death in yours

One day perhaps I'll learn to hear
     the hidden laugh
                under your blue cascades
to live on and love you better
and carry you along till the end

SAID ONCE MORE THAT *IT* MAY NEVER COME TO PASS

During

There will not be so much as a man's look left,
nor do I know if women will still have eyes.
But I do know that at the finish
across blocks of stone scorched
                              to the heart
        — for these were cities —
there will sweep like the revolving beam
        of some terrible lighthouse
                the terrifying
                astonished
irradiated gaze of a child
seeking the shadow of a god
                              among the ruins.

After

There was
there is
there will be
maybe
— for nothing is less certain than the lifetime of
      things
in this moment of the world wherein I speak to you —
a blade of grass still pushing up
among the stumps and stones
when there's nothing else left at all
but that one green blade
            with one little thought
                    in its green head.

II

THIS DESERT NOW

Night Phrases

In this unprecedented night, the sun alone cannot
    suffice
for the thickness of lost time awaits me
    at every turning.

I have wrecked so many gardens where I had dreamed
    of blooming
and smashed so many mirrors where I thought to find
    the others,
only to see always my own face leering back at me,
that my life is now strewn with the shards of myself
like a trail of evil ruins.

Somehow I could not find the road towards the
    warmth of the other
and I lost sight of the sun
while behind me
    time went on thickening.

Every day now I travel a little farther from myself
leaving the straight path   home   friends
    a woman
and the fruits of speech
on my way towards death in a place where finally
    nothing
will remind me of who I am
where finally nothing will look like anything else.

In Order Not to Go Away

In this rock
in the thickness of this rock,
in the ultimate death of roots,
in the absence of a threshold,
and this petrification even of necessary water,

I navigate.

In the fire,
in the finish of this fire,
not far from my eyes,
in the finish of this body
closer than this rock
at the end of my eyes,

I navigate,
immobile,
at the bottom of black stones.

II

Peopled with strangenesses,
assailed by the parallels of shadow
in a hot and funerary solstice,
I lack the strength
                    to cry out.
I have nothing
            of what must happen to me
in order
        not
            to go away.

I Am Not Seeing What I See

I am not seeing what I see
and I see nothing of what is
not finding there the things I seek.

I am not hearing what I hear
and I hear nothing of all that sings
not finding there what I expected.

I am not feeling what I feel
and I see nothing that resembles
an ellipse in any way.

I am not feeling what I ought
and I feel nothing of what would be
the chosen pathway of a god

or the works of pillage in some new war.

But I do taste   oh how keenly
this savour of ashes
which in my veins has replaced the beating blood

I see nothing   I hear nothing   I feel nothing.

I taste only these mortal ashes.

And they have not the sweetness I invented
    for the death of everyone.

Lost Ways that Somewhere
Wind Together

For Monique Dussault

I

The trouble is having been born on this blood-stained and ill-omened planet, dead already without knowing it, playing out for itself a comedy of life.

This is no joke.

But nonetheless we can carry on scribbling and sketching while awaiting the return of the Great Sorceries.

II

I fail to see why I should return to waste my life here on this side of images, where the rest of you are making so much noise.

I would much rather lose my way in the traces of a sun hiding behind its own death spots.

III

I tunnelled so many walls, like the irradiated mole of some future war, I threaded so many labyrinths flickering before me like jellyfish, I tunnelled so far, day and night, really like something seen in images, *that I found myself outside.*

It was cold there, cold as the centre of god.
But it was warm there too, warm as the centre of god.

And I think it was at that moment that I lost sight of the rest of you.

IV

I am the dream of an immobile stratum, witness to the passage of the great primal sorceries, magic with their hordes of words, those that forged this world as it now appears and the unspokenness of the palpable.

But time, but the weariness of the species, but the accident that I am, have finished me.

How to find my way in this criss-crossing of tracks? How to tell the true sign from the mirage, the real word from the noisy, coloured illusion?

V

We had not lost our way on the same roads, but lost ways somewhere wind together.

At least that's what I hear in the wind when I still hear anything at all.

That's what I see when, for an instant, my blindness lifts.

VI

For so long I walked those frontiers where words and images are strewn in shipwreck.

And I cried out so loud and long that I burst even the echo of echo.

I had almost reached the heart when I lost my own tracks, *out there*.

Sometimes it seems to you that I am here.
In reality, I never came back.

VII

It was then that I met the woman of my life, a Sorceress from the dead stars.

Never shall I tell you the secret she gave me.

For I have no more time for talking.

Besides, why would I talk and what should I say amongst you, living in an uproar that has long since deafened you, killed you, separated you from yourselves and from the sap of the star and the blood of the sacred animal?

Truly, I have no more time for talking.

I have no more time for wasting time.

For with my Sorceress from the dead stars I am improvising a music of death and a dance of life, both peopled with fables and masks.

I leave it to you to guess what they conceal.

VIII

No, don't go away so quickly. I wasn't saying these things to take my leave of you.

Tell me who you are.
Make me a sign.
Make of me your sign.

Perhaps you are the very one, the sign I have been waiting for.

The Transmutation of the Blind

For Louise-Esther Fortin,
my dark elf-woman.

I

I am blind and yet I see you.
I am deaf and yet I hear
the murmurs rising from your eyes.

The cry tore you open like a knife of ice
and I was not there.
I do not know where the black winds come from.
I do not know if this day will be shipwrecked.
But I do know that you are like the shadow
that gives birth to a sun
sign and beacon against the thickness of things.

I know that you will come
before the fire collapses into the cold water.

II

Do not reject
what the night has to teach you.

And the changeless wound
do not cover it with a mask
which later will crumble away
revealing it deeper still
rather than more beautiful.

Do not reject
what the night has to teach you.
But do not linger
where vain death blends with night,
for there are two kinds of death
and the other confers greatness on him who harbours
        her,
    like a child of nights grown sleepless with light.

III

Those who strike when they would have caressed.
Those who break down doors opening onto nothing.
Those who break themselves upon the Great Door
        which opens upon the dawning of things.
Those who break themselves for nothing.
Those who break themselves for everything, like the
        child of a nocturnal anger
who might be divine in the name of all children dead
        in us.

They are the ones who will recognize each other by
        the looks
they cast upon their ruins and their fruits.

We shall lose sight of them for they will be too far
        ahead,
at the threshold of the primal fire that reigns far from
        here.

IV

I am blind and yet I see you.
I am deaf and yet I hear you.

Do not reject
what the day has to teach you.
Make of it the food of your hours
and do not forget the hunger of him you hate,
and do not forget the thirst of him who loves you
but whom you do not see.
Feed him with luminous gestures
and honey will sweeten the murderous word
in your mouth open at last to the true breath
barely living in you
because you have not yet fashioned the heart
        of your retreat
with the scattered pieces of yourself.

Know how to be blind and see nothing
and you will see.
Know how to be deaf and to hear only
the founding song
which resounds where the verb to love
mingles with time.

And music then, all the musics of this world
and of the Opus will be yours
like a sheaf of knowledge.

Non-Lieu

We who are from here but without being here
and who are from elsewhere while being neither here
    nor there.
We who are from elsewhere while actually being
    there, and losing ourselves there,
and who are from here but are powerless to stay.

We who are from here but powerless, and who are
    also elsewhere but just barely,
and who are here and powerless to be elsewhere.
We who are from elsewhere and powerless to remain
    there
and who are from everywhere and powerless to stop.
We who are from everywhere and powerless to be
    elsewhere
and who are from everywhere and powerless to be
    here,
and who are from here without actually being here
because no one ever stays here without dying.

But we who do not wish to die unless we are too tired
    to remain.
We who are going to die at the precise moment
    when....
We who shall remain from now on, here or
    elsewhere,
unable to go on and die farther along,

unable to go on and die everywhere at the same time
and how beautiful that would be.

We who are there, do you see, without being there,
because you did not know how to look,
and who are, although others are not,
and who still are, without the others.

But precisely, we precisely who are nothing
without the others, and who are, even in the absence
of the others,
and who are not happy when the others are not there.

We, precisely, we who are never anything
unless the others are too.
But we, precisely, we who never arrive anywhere
unless the others are already there to stop all that.

What are we going to beco....
Yes — the question — the only question —
And really the only one left to be asked.
To be asked of the stones because men no longer
answer
the questions that are asked of them.

We have some idea of where we come from but not
much.
You have no better idea than before of who you are.
They have no idea of where they are going.

So what are we going to beco....

In the first place, do we want to go — I mean
do we want to go somewhere or don't we?
Or is there nothing we want — I mean
to go nowhere or what?
Or what, I mean, where?

When it comes down to it, I don't know, I'm just
        talking.
What does it mean, we who
we who precisely
we who are from here without being here
        because no one ever stays here without dying.

We who.... But what were you just saying?
We who.... What? I just don't understand.
We who.... But what is all this?
We who.... But who's that knocking at the door?
There are no doors here. We are completely free.
All doors are open. Even if heads are closed.
So who is knocking what?

Who is knocking whom because I can hear
        in the distance and coming closer
        a sound sometimes dull and sometimes sharp
                and which I recognize
                        and which reminds me...
                                but of what?

Ah, we who are without really being really,
we who are or are not,
what is going to become, yes,
what is going to become of us?

Prayer in Simple Prose

For Sébastien, my distant son, who will perhaps understand one day... if he survives on this planet which has gone mad.

In the name of the contradiction of the Father and of the Son, of the Mother and of the Daughter, and of the improbable Spirit which has made of them what they are.

In the name of war and of peace, of destruction and creation, in the name of those for whom we can do nothing, and in the name of ourselves for whom we can do very little, in the name of those for whom we shall never be able to do more than what we are, than what we have made of ourselves.

In the name of what they have done with us, undone in us.

In the name of the road we have left to travel.

For nothing or for everything.

In the name of that nothing and of that everything.

In the name of the very name of all things dead and beautiful and of the living.

In the name of lost prophets wandering roads no longer recognized.

In the name of the Mother gone mad in herself, for herself, by herself.

In the name of the peace-loving Father who through habit or necessity has become someone's warrior enemy.

In the name of the Son and of the Daughter whom I disliked because of the noise that children make, and whom now I contemplate with greater worry than before when I consider what is, for I see it already beginning to resemble what awaits us.

In the name of the Son and of the Daughter.
In the name of their dog.
In the name of their toys, imbued with the sound of their voices, their joys, their angers and their tears, toys destined to finish their days alone, but filled with the soul of the children, in some dark corner of a forgotten room. Yet more alone in the smoke of the ruins. And yet more alone when there are no children left, but only a few blackened playthings strewn over a desert streaked with strange flashes and blasted with great winds.

In the name of the refusal of what exists.

In the name of the refusal of what is coming and of what will probably be with us for a long time.

In the name of the Water, condemned to death, of the Earth and of everything it bears of nourishment and splendour, in the name of the Air, condemned to death, and of Fire, instrument of death become again an act of kindness.

In the name of the Name which has lost its name in the disordered noise of things.

In the name of the Name which finds its meaning once again in the absence of a name.

In the name of the Name that I find again when I love, although I do not love enough. And when I love enough, I love badly. And when I love badly, I panic about the quality of that Name of which I speak and which I long to know, to experience as one knows the soul of a weapon in battle. And thus I find war again, which is not what I want.

And therefore, in my name, I distance myself from that name and from that weapon and I turn away, with somewhat fewer illusions than before, towards the Son and the Mother, the Daughter and the Father and the Spirit I am seeking — in the name of — but of what exactly?

So be it, as anyone else might say.
But I say:
So should it not be.

It would have been better if nothing had ever become what is.

An Absence

'I'll wait for you,' he said.

And she left. She didn't come back. He waited so long for her that he lost sight of himself.

When she did come back, she had wandered so widely all over the world that she was no longer able to reassemble the parts of herself.

They met again (chance, destiny, blind luck or bad luck).

And she asked too politely, looking away,

'How are you?'

He looked away.

'How do you want me to be?' he said, listlessly. 'I'm no longer going anywhere and I'm no longer here. I waited so long. The stones you see there are younger than I am. And you?'

'I travelled so far that I'm having trouble gathering up the pieces of myself that I scattered across the world.'

'Then how is the world?'

'Oh, the world, the world... you know the world... it's like you and me. And so the world, you see, has not much future.'

Short Memoir of an October Night

I arrived without announcing myself, serious as a stone, full of high words but already broken by the slightest absence of love, and yet swaggering like a rat in the darkest navigations, the far corners of strange ports.

In spite of that I climbed the tree that would be struck by lightning.

I survived. I had survived even childhood, that living sepulchre.

When I left, very early, I wanted them to call me back, although I let it seem that I was turning away. But I longed, I longed to be called back. So as not to fall.

But no one called me. Or if someone did, I didn't hear it.

Since that time, I am falling. I never finish falling.

*

Falling would be nothing, were it not for the slowness of the descent. For then the weight of self, yes, the weight becomes a terrible thing to carry.

But there is no choice. This we must carry to the grave, this weight heavier than earth must be buried in the Earth already so heavy to bear.

*

I am losing all sense of proportion.... In truth, it is not so much the Earth as its men and women who have become very heavy. They are now much too heavy for the Earth which, in itself, is so light....

They have become so heavy that the Earth will also fall. Where, I do not know, but the Earth will fall, that is sure.

*

This desert now.

This burial in the earth. (*Burial in the earth*: we must also dig into the meaning of these words.)

But the worst is not the burial in the earth. No. That is nothing.

The worst is *burial in the desert*, knowing already what the Earth is worth and the worth of what it bears upon it, and that nothing else is left, just that, the desert, for a place to put oneself at last.

A Gravitation Vaguely Zen

Sometimes I've dreamed of conquering Space with the ponderous, powerful, complicated machines invented by my brothers and myself, too long ago already.

Those were children with the sun behind them, far behind, as stubbornly they gauged the long and frozen night stretching to the four corners of being and the world. And always with an idea like a nail, an idea like a hammer upon the nail, the idea of going farther than this Space, this night too long; the idea of a long, long journey shot through with comets in mad parabolas and straight lines to the heart of things.

All that should be left behind in the serenity of the coming ruins. Some at least, from the less sombre side of the House of Aquarius, think that.

But the ponderous, powerful, complicated machines are precisely too much of what they are.

We would have to concentrate *forces*, give the necessary souls to beautiful things like wings, and economize *internal gravitation*.

I can hear you already, laughing like dogs yapping.

But I'm telling you. We could conquer Space on our windsurfers, on our loveliest sailboats, on hang-gliders, on the velvety flight of ultimate synergy.

Yet you laugh, pirates, philosophers, policemen.... You laugh like dogs yapping, circling nastily round the subject and never biting into it.

*

The worst, in the gravitation of being and of things, is when one reaches *the centre*.
What a weight.
The enormous weight of things at their centre.
The black hole.
The black hole of things at their extreme centre.

And no one. No one to tell us where this power is going, the Force of things, concentrated upon itself to the point of explosion.

*

'You ask me the stupidest of questions, dear thing, oh excuse me.... Dear friend.... Would you prefer *dear being*? Did you know that between the being and the thing, the question is merely one of perception? You believe that you *are*, therefore that you are as you perceive *the thing*. But nothing, absolutely nothing can certify for you that *the thing*, looking back at you, does not take itself for *a being*. And there are always certain things that you will break, taking them for what you know of them as things, but without ever imagining that there might exist somewhere in them a little bit of *being*.

'There are, however, many things that can also break you, mistaking you for a being, or even a similar thing. And that is certainly the pinnacle of atrocity — that a being, or perhaps a thing, whatever the nature of its methods, should break you because it takes you for a being, or even a thing, whatever the case may be, or worse, because it takes you for what you are: one of its fellows.'

Whoever is speaking to me can only be standing against the light.

And now he is silent, but the music of his words lulls me long after.

When he turns towards me, he removes from his face, or at least from what I thought was his face, a mask, then another, then two, then three, then a hundred masks, all of which look just like us, like you and me.

*

Somewhere, tomorrow or the day after, I shall have discovered the tragedy of the past of my species.

What a road to reach that point....

Long ago, an old, great and perverse philosopher ('I hate you as much as I love you', wrote Baudelaire in quite different circumstances) said that of... but who was it he was speaking of ?

I shall have discovered that I am a circle whose centre is everywhere and whose circumference is nowhere....

A circle whose centre

everywhere

circumference

nowhere

a circle-centre

everywhere

circumference

centre

everywhere

centre

Waiting

For Paul-Marie Lapointe,
because of the Apocalypse...

I really was waiting for the Word to be made flesh;
I laboured hard and sternly at that Opus.
But I was following a star which was dead and
     unsustainable,
and living in the adoration of an Image....

When I lost my faith, I lived through Hell.
It was very much like the death of metaphor,
of metonymy, of catachresis
and all those wise conceits.

Although the apocalypse was purely rhetorical.

Biographical Note

Yves Préfontaine was born in Montréal in 1937 and published his first poems at the age of fifteen. A natural musician, for many years he was host of a Radio-Canada jazz programme, Jazz-Sortilèges, and was actively involved in jazz promotion as well as in writing and publishing. His work for Radio-Canada and Radio-Canada International was to include the writing and presentation of radio series on *L'Homme américain* (the native peoples of North America), on black literature from Africa and the West Indies, and on contemporary writers and composers. In addition to his broadcasting career, a lifelong passion for botany and geology has led him on what he describes as a cosmological quest, a search to understand his relations with all dimensions of space.

In 1959, at the age of eighteen, after collaborating in the founding of the magazines *Situations* and *Québec Libre*, he joined the editorial board of the magazine *Liberté* and was its editor-in-chief in 1961-1962. Deeply disturbed by the problems of language and culture which he observed around him in Montreal, he was early committed to the sovereignist struggle. It was in 1964 that his apartment was entered and ransacked by the police for the first time.

Always fascinated by the lives and traditions of the aboriginal peoples of America, in 1957-1958, he lived and travelled in Mexico, returning slowly through the United States in a search for geographical roots and his own *américanité française*. In 1962, he enrolled in an M.A. in anthropology at l'Université de Montréal and went from there to Paris to do doctoral work at l'École pratique des Hautes études from 1966 to 1970. During this period he seized the opportunity to explore Western and Eastern Europe and North Africa, in addition to working on French radio.

When he arrived back in Montréal in 1970, it was just in time for the War Measures Act. Held at gunpoint by a soldier in his apartment, he was to overhear a Montréal policeman explaining to the military that 'this one isn't really very dangerous; he works for *les Anglais...*', because he had just been hired to teach at McGill. Thus he was not arrested. His political commitment, however, was deepened and strengthened by the sense of enormous insult that the experience left with him.

Since that time, Yves Préfontaine's interests have led him to work in communications for the Government of Québec, for the Québec Ministry of Education and for educational television. In the 1970s he was Chef de Cabinet for the Québec Minister of State for Cultural Development. He won the Prix du Congrès du Spectacle in 1963 and in 1968 he won the Prix France-Québec as well as first prize in the Concours Littéraires du Québec for his fourth book, *Pays sans parole*. Currently he does consultation and research for the Québec Ministry of Higher Education and Science. He divides his time between his home in Outremont and his cottage on Lake Champlain. He says that he needs the contact with the real soil and 'to get his feet in the water' in order to write.

This Desert Now is his most recent work and represents the culmination of his explorations so far.

*

* *

Born on Cape Breton Island but raised and educated in Toronto, Judith Cowan studied at the University of Toronto, as well as in France and in Québec. She is a longtime translator of Québec poets. The magazine *Ellipse* has published most of her single-poem translations and others have appeared in *Le Sabord*, *Les Écrits des Forges*, *Arc*, *Matrix* and Columbia University's *Journal of Literary Translation*. Her first book-length translation was of Yolande Villemaire's *Quartz and Mica* (Guernica, 1987).

Her own poems, written in either English or French, have appeared in *Matrix*, *Arc*, *English Today*, *En vrac*, *Le Beffroi*, and *Liberté*.

Judith Cowan teaches English literature to Québecois students at l'Université du Québec à Trois-Rivières and, at the moment, is working on a collection of short stories.

Printed by
Ateliers Graphiques Marc Veilleux Inc.
Cap-Saint-Ignace (Québec)
in August 1993